Mexico

ELAINE LANDAU

Children's Press®
An Imprint of Scholastic Inc.
New York Toronto London Auckland Sydney
Mexico City New Delhi Hong Kong
Danbury, Connecticut

Content Consultant
Hannah H. Covert
Executive Director
Center for Latin American Studies
University of Florida
Gainesville, Florida

Library of Congress Cataloging-in-Publication Data

Landau, Elaine.
Mexico / by Elaine Landau.
p. cm. -- (A true book)
Includes bibliographical references and index.
ISBN-13: 978-0-531-16853-0 (lib. bdg.)
978-0-531-20727-7 (pbk.)
ISBN-10: 0-531-16853-0 (lib. bdg.)
0-531-20727-7 (pbk.)

1. Mexico--Juvenile literature. I. Title. II. Series.

F1208.5.L26 2007
972--dc22 2007036024

Produced by Weldon Owen Education Inc.

1 2 3 4 5 6 7 8 9 10 R 17 16 15 14 13 12 11 10 09 08

Find the Truth!

Everything you are about to read is true ***except*** for one of the sentences on this page.

Which one is **TRUE**?

T or F Large groups of Komodo dragons live in parts of Mexico.

T or F Pink flamingos and brightly colored parrots live in Mexico.

Find the answers in this book.

Contents

Scarlet macaws are large parrots found in Mexico. They have a very loud scream!

The green iguana is a lizard. It is found in southern Mexico. Komodo (kuh-MOH-doh) dragons are lizards too. However, you won't find any in Mexico. They live only in Indonesia.

CHAPTER 1

Let's Go to Mexico

Your plane has just landed in Mexico City. Your trip to Mexico has begun! In Mexico, there are rain forests and there are beaches. There are cities and mountains. There are monkeys and iguanas. A sampling of a lot of different places and experiences seems like a good idea.

An iguana is a reptile. Mexico has more than 700 kinds of reptiles.

Cruise the City and Country

Most of Mexico's people live in cities. Mexico City is the capital and largest city. The city has mountains and volcanoes on all sides. Ancient ruins have been **excavated** right in the middle of the city! There are more than 100 museums. Aztec pyramids are a short trip from the center.

The greater Mexico City area has a population of nearly 20 million. It is the second most populated city after Tokyo.

Tulum is an ancient Mayan walled city. It is found in southeast Mexico.

You certainly don't want to miss Mexico's historical sites. There are ruins of ancient cities along the coast. Others are buried deep in the rain forests. The remains of temples and pyramids are many hundreds of years old.

Every year, thousands of tourists flock to Acapulco on the Pacific Coast of Mexico. It is famous for its beaches and brave cliff divers.

A Neighbor Nation

Cliff divers in Acapulco dive from as high as 120 feet (37 meters).

Mexico sits between very different neighbors. Mexico's neighbor to the north is the United States. The two countries are separated by the Rio Grande river. Mexico's neighbors to the southeast are Belize and Guatemala. Mexico sits at the northern end of Central America.

From Coast to Coast

Look at the map of Mexico. The country is shaped a little like a dolphin's tail. Much of Mexico is bounded by water. The Pacific Ocean is on its west coast. The Gulf of Mexico and the Caribbean Sea are to its east.

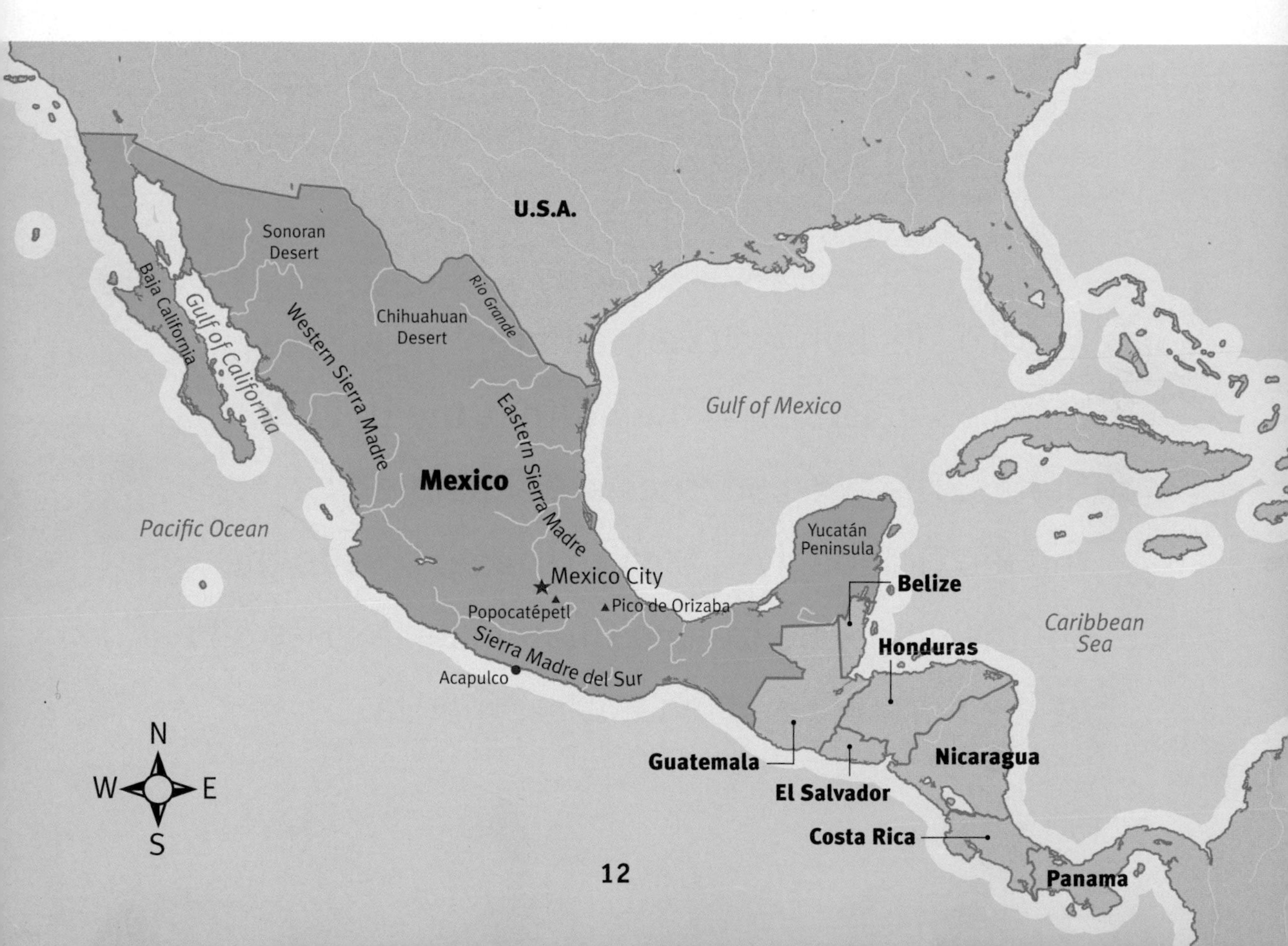

At the southeast end of Mexico is the Yucatán (yoo-kah-TAN) **Peninsula**. The Yucatán is known for its rain forests and white, sandy beaches. It is also home to the Yucatecan Mayan people. They are the largest **indigenous** population in North America. The Maya have lived in the Yucatán for thousands of years.

The ruins of Chichén Itzá (chee-CHEHN eet-SAH) are on the Yucatán Peninsula. Maya still live in the area.

Thousands of pink flamingos live in reserves in the Yucatán.

There is desert in northern Mexico. Along the two coasts are mountain ranges called the Western and Eastern Sierra Madre. Between these ranges lies a high region called the **Plateau** of Mexico. The area has many volcanoes and lakes. It also has the nation's most **fertile** soil. Much of Mexico's population lives on this plateau. Mexico City is there.

Mexico is famous for silverware, such as vases and jewelry.

Made in Mexico

Mexico is rich in natural minerals. It is the world's largest producer of silver. The country also mines copper, lead, gold, zinc, salt, and sulfur. Mexico began producing oil in the early 1900s. Today, **petroleum** is a major export.

Manufacturing is important to Mexico's economy too. A large number of Mexicans work in factories. Cars, chemicals, office equipment, and steel are among Mexico's leading products.

Mexico's Income

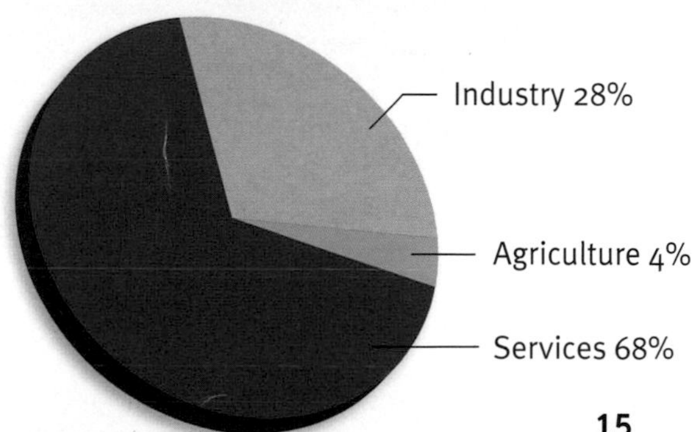

Mexico's national income comes mainly from services related to tourism. These include hotels, restaurants, and transportation.

Only about 12 percent of Mexico's land is used for farming. In most places, the soil is too dry or rocky. Yet Mexico still produces a great deal of corn, coffee, oranges, sugarcane, and cacao (kuh-KOU) beans.

Though Mexico produces many products, it has some problems too. While some Mexicans are wealthy, many workers are very poorly paid. Each year, thousands of Mexicans cross the border to the United States to look for work.

One cacao tree produces enough beans every year to make five pounds of chocolate.

Oh, No, Popo!

Have you ever seen a volcano up close? There are about 3,000 volcanoes in Mexico. Popocatépetl (poh-puh-kah-TEP-ehtl) is just southeast of Mexico City. Most Mexicans just call it Popo. Popo is Mexico's second-highest volcano. The highest is Pico de Orizaba.

Since the 1300s, Popo has erupted about 30 times. It spews out gas, ash, smoke, and steam. Luckily, most of Popo's recent eruptions have been small!

The Olmec people carved stone heads. The heads weighed as much as 36,000 pounds (16,300 kilograms) each.

CHAPTER 3

From the Past to the Present

From about 1500 B.C. to 1500 A.D., many great Native American civilizations lived in the Mexico area. These included the Olmec, Maya, Zapotec, Toltec, and Aztec. The Spanish arrived in Mexico more than 500 years ago. Their arrival changed the course of Mexican history.

The Olmec left behind huge stone heads. Some heads are as tall as 11 feet (3.3 meters).

Ancient Empires

The Maya lived in Mexico from about 1000 B.C. to 1500 A.D. The ruins of their magnificent pyramids and temples can be seen today. The Maya were advanced in mathematics and astronomy.

During the 1400s and early 1500s, parts of Mexico were ruled by the Aztec empire. The Aztec were great **architects** and engineers. Their cities had palaces, parks, and marketplaces. They founded the Aztec capital Tenochtitlán (teh-nohch-teet-LAHN). This is the site of present-day Mexico City.

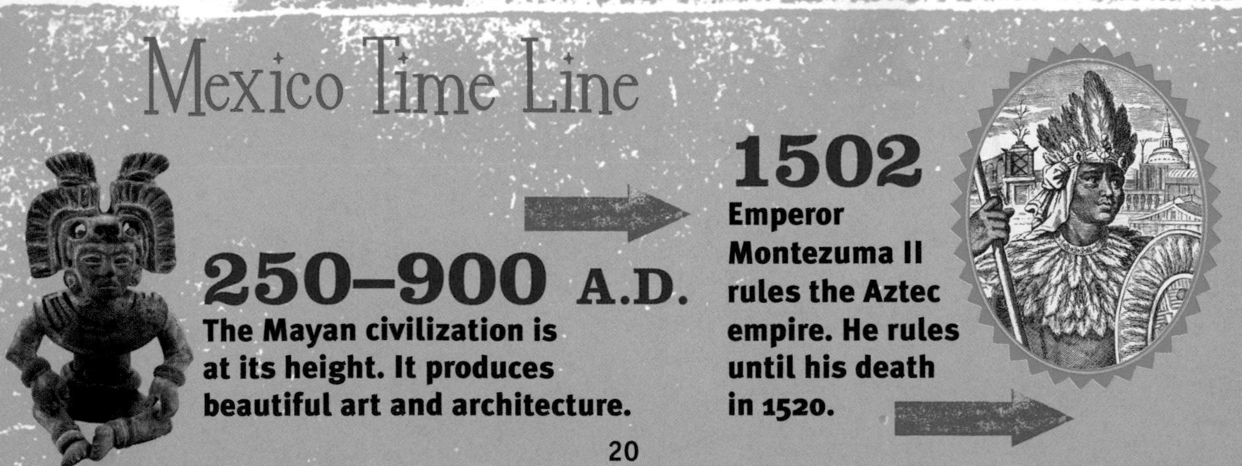

Mexico Time Line

250–900 A.D.
The Mayan civilization is at its height. It produces beautiful art and architecture.

1502
Emperor Montezuma II rules the Aztec empire. He rules until his death in 1520.

The Spanish Invasion

Life changed for the Aztecs in 1519. That was when Hernando Cortés of Spain landed in Mexico. In three years, Cortés and his soldiers tore down the Aztec cities. They took Aztec people as slaves. Millions of Aztec were killed by soldiers. Many died from diseases the Spanish carried. They had no natural **immunity**.

In 1521, Mexico became a Spanish **colony**. Spain ruled Mexico for 300 years. Yet the indigenous peoples longed for freedom.

War and More

In 1810, the local people **rebelled** against the Spanish. The Mexican War of Independence lasted until 1821. Finally, Mexico was free of Spain's control.

However, the next hundred years brought many more battles. Mexico lost almost half its territory to the United States. Texas was claimed in 1845. By 1848, the Mexican War was over. That year, Mexico received $15 million for land in the northwest.

In 1853, the United States paid $10 million for land in what is now New Mexico and southern Arizona.

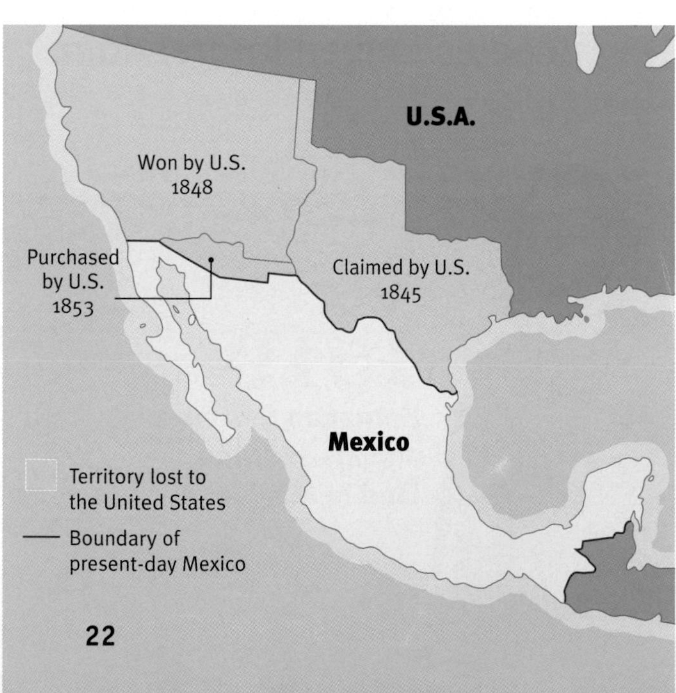

The Mexican Revolution

During the 1800s, Mexico had harsh rulers. Just a few wealthy families owned most of Mexico's land. This angered the peasants. They went to war in 1910. More than a million Mexicans died during the Mexican Revolution.

In 1917, a new **constitution** was formed. Mexico was divided into 31 states. A new president would be elected every six years. The government started giving more land and rights to workers.

Emilio Zapata was a leading fighter in the Mexican Revolution. His soldiers were called Zapatistas.

Columns Galore

The Plaza of a Thousand Columns may have been used as a marketplace. Each column is about 8 feet (2.5 meters) high. It is believed that the plaza originally had a thatched roof.

THE BIG TRUTH!

Pyramid of Power

Chichén Itzá is on the Yucatán Peninsula. It was the most important Mayan city between about 900 and 1200 A.D. It has been named one of the New Seven Wonders of the World. The heart of the city is the Pyramid of Kukulkan. Other structures include raised platforms, an observatory, and a huge ball court.

Special Numbers

The limestone pyramid is 75 feet (23 meters) tall. It has 91 steps on each of its four sides. If you count the platform on top, there are 365 steps altogether. That equals the number of days in a year. There are also 18 terraces on each side. These represent the 18 months of the Mayan calendar.

Sacred Sounds

The ball court is 545 feet (166 meters) long. It is 225 feet (68 meters) wide. It has unusual qualities. When you whisper at one end of the court, you can clearly hear the words at the other end. If you make a sound in the center of the court, it will produce nine echoes.

Mexican masks are usually made of wood. They can also be made of shells and tin. Some have real hair and teeth!

CHAPTER 4

Art at the Heart of Mexico

Mexican mask dances are usually performed only by men. They play both male and female characters.

From paintings to handicrafts to buildings, Mexican art bursts with color. Mask making has been a tradition for centuries. The pre-**Hispanic** cultures used masks in religious ceremonies. After the Spanish arrived, masks were also used in some Christian ceremonies.

This mural by Diego Rivera is on a theater building in Mexico City.

Proud Painters

The Maya and the Aztec left behind large carvings and pictures of gods and animals on temple walls. Modern Mexican artists also painted murals. Three artists became especially well known for their murals following the Mexican Revolution of 1910. They were Diego Rivera, David Siqueiros, and José Orozco. Their paintings tell the history of Mexico.

Frida Kahlo was also a famous Mexican painter. She was seriously injured in an accident when she was fifteen years old. Her self-portraits depict her pain as well as her pride in being Mexican. Kahlo married Diego Rivera in 1929.

Rufino Tamayo was another outstanding artist. His paintings are richly colorful. He used handmade paper to achieve a rough texture.

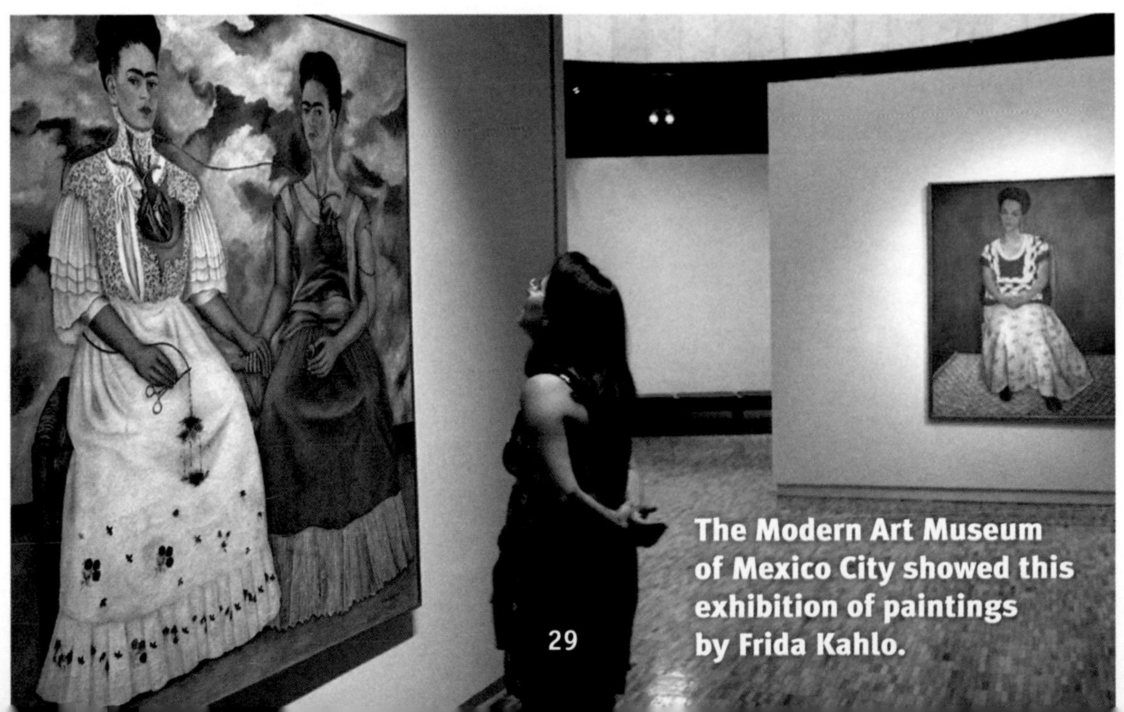

The Modern Art Museum of Mexico City showed this exhibition of paintings by Frida Kahlo.

Colorful Crafts

Mexico has produced talented craftspeople. The Aztec made necklaces, bracelets, and nose jewelry out of gold and copper. Today, Mexican craftspeople are known for their pottery and silver jewelry. They also make colorful, handwoven cloth and wall hangings.

Music is an important part of Mexican culture. Mexican mariachi bands are easy to spot. These strolling musicians play guitars, violins, and trumpets. Wearing their large-brimmed hats, they perform in restaurants and on streets.

The Mexican hat dance is a popular folk dance. The dance ends with the couple pretending to kiss behind the hat!

Folk-dance dresses are brightly colored. They have lots of ribbons and petticoats.

Food is an important part of the Day of the Dead celebration. Families prepare many tasty dishes and sweet treats.

CHAPTER 5

Fiestas and Food

Mexicans love fiestas, or parties. Like most cultures, Mexico has special days of celebration. The Day of the Dead is on the first two days of November. This is not a sad time. It is a time for Mexicans to pay respect to their ancestors. Family graves are decorated with candles and flowers. Some people dress up in costumes.

On the Day of the Dead, children enjoy skull-shaped candy!

On December 12, Guadalupe (gwah-duh-LOOP) Day is Mexico's most religious holiday. People honor the Virgin of Guadalupe, Mexico's **patron saint**. It is said that about 475 years ago, she appeared to a peasant named Juan Diego. She told him that she wanted a church to be built where she stood. Thousands of Mexicans visit this chapel in Mexico City on Guadalupe Day.

The patron saint is also known as Our Lady of Guadalupe.

Many people dance in parades on Independence Day.

In Mexico, Independence Day is celebrated on September 16. There are big parades and firework displays.

Cinco de Mayo means "Fifth of May" in Spanish. On May 5, 1862, Mexicans fought off French soldiers in the city of Puebla. Today, proud Mexicans in all parts of the world hold celebrations on this day.

Nice With Spice

Mexican food is spicy and delicious. Tortillas are thin, flat bread. They are made from ground corn or wheat flour. Tacos are a crisp, fried tortilla. Both may be eaten with meat or beans. They are often topped with cheese and chilies. Enchiladas are stuffed tortillas baked in sauce. For dessert, many Mexicans love flan, a custard with a soft caramel topping. Another treat is a drink of spiced hot chocolate.

Chocolate is whipped to a foamy froth with a carved wooden stick called a *molinillo*.

According to traditional belief, the spirit of hot chocolate is in the foam.

Party Time!

Going to a birthday party? You may find a Mexican piñata there. A piñata is a colorful container filled with candy and small toys. It can be shaped like a star, an animal, or a flower. At a party, the piñata is hung high in a tree out of reach. Then children are blindfolded. They take turns trying to hit the piñata with a stick. When it breaks, the candy and toys fall out. Hurry, everyone! Grab the treats!

Mexico's flag features an eagle, a cactus, and a snake. The flag's colors stand for independence (green), religion (white), and union (red).

CHAPTER 6

Life in Mexico

A legend says that the Aztec built their city where they saw an eagle perched on a cactus, eating a snake.

"¿Habla español?" That means, "Do you speak Spanish?" Spanish is Mexico's official language. Before the Spanish arrived, different native groups spoke their own languages. More than 60 native languages are still spoken in Mexico. However, Spanish is the language that unites all Mexicans.

Faith, Family, and Fun

The Spanish also brought the Catholic religion to Mexico. **Missionaries** arrived early on to convert the native population. As the Spanish and native peoples intermarried, their cultures became mixed. These Mexicans are known as mestizos. Today, about 90 percent of Mexicans are Roman Catholic.

Most Mexican weddings take place in a Roman Catholic church. In villages, the bride is paraded down the main street.

It is customary for a Mexican groom to give his wife a present of 13 gold coins.

Having lunch at a restaurant is a favorite family outing on a Sunday.

Some Mexican households are large. Often a household is not simply parents with their children. Grandparents, aunts, uncles, and cousins may live with them too.

Many children throughout Mexico attend free public schools. There are also private schools for those who can afford them. All Mexican children are required to go to school until they are at least fourteen years old.

Many Mexican children enjoy sports. *Fútbol* (soccer) is the national sport. *Béisbol* (baseball) and basketball are also popular.

Some day, you may take a trip to Mexico. Now you know more about its history, geography, art, and food. You can plan a great visit! ★

True Statistics

Proper name: Estados Unidos Mexicanos (United Mexican States)

Official language: Spanish

Area: 756,066 sq mi (1,958,201 sq km)

Population: About 108.7 million

Major religion: Roman Catholic

Type of government: Federal republic

Head of government: President

Capital and largest city: Mexico City

Money: Mexican peso

Weights and measures: Metric system

Seaports: More than 30

Did you find the truth?

F Large groups of Komodo dragons live in parts of Mexico.

T Pink flamingos and brightly colored parrots live in Mexico.

Resources

Books

Asher, Sandy. *Mexico*. Tarrytown, NY: Benchmark Books, 2003.

Fontes, Justine and Ron. *Mexico* (A to Z Series). Children's Press, 2003. New York:

Ganeri, Anita. *Ancient Maya*. Minneapolis: Compass Point Books, 2006.

Lourie, Peter. *The Hidden World of the Aztec*. Honesdale, PA: Boyds Mills Press, 2006.

Lowery, Linda. *Day of the Dead*. Minneapolis: Carolrhoda Books, 2004.

Morrison, Marion. *Mexico City*. Milwaukee: World Almanac Library, 2004.

Sheen, Barbara. *Foods of Mexico*. Detroit: KidHaven Press, 2006.

Stein, R. Conrad. *Hernando Cortés: Conquistador and Empire Builder*. Mankato, MN: The Child's World, 2004.

Stout, Mary. *Aztec*. Milwaukee: Gareth Stevens, 2004.

Venezia, Mike. *Frida Kahlo*. New York: Children's Press, 1999.

Organizations and Web Sites

Mayan Kids
www.mayankids.com
Learn about Mayan people, places, and beliefs, such as the Day of the Dead.

The Aztec Calendar
www.azteccalendar.com
Find out more about the calendar developed by the Aztecs.

Make a Piñata
www.dltk-kids.com/world/mexico/simple_paper_bag_pinata.htm
Learn how to make a piñata out of a paper bag.

Places to Visit

The National Museum of Mexican Art
1852 West 19th Street
Chicago, IL 60608
312-738-1503
www.nationalmuseumofmexicanart.org
Learn more about Mexican history, culture, and performing arts.

The Mexican Museum
Fort Mason Center
Building D
San Francisco, CA 94123
415-202-9700
www.mexicanmuseum.org
Explore five areas of Mexican art from pre-Hispanic to modern artists.

Important Words

architect (AR-kuh-tekt) – a person who designs buildings and directs their construction

colony (KOL-uh-nee) – a settlement under the rule of a parent country

constitution – the rules by which a government is run

excavate – to dig out

fertile (FUR-tuhl) – rich and good for plants to grow in

Hispanic – relating to Spain or Spanish-speaking Latin America

immunity – the body's ability to fight off disease

indigenous (in-DIJ-uh-nuhs) – the original people living in an area

missionary – a person sent by a religious group to teach that religion to others

patron saint – a saint that is believed to offer protection to a particular country or cause

peninsula – a narrow strip of land nearly surrounded by water

petroleum – a thick, oily liquid used to make gasoline

plateau (pla-TOH) – an area of high, flat land

rebel – to fight against authority or those in charge

Index

About the Author

Award-winning author Elaine Landau has a bachelor's degree from New York University and a master's degree in Library and Information Science. She has written more than 300 nonfiction books for children and young adults.

Elaine likes to travel and has visited Mexico many times. She loves the people and has spent many happy hours on the beach in Cozumel.

When she's not traveling, Elaine lives in Miami, Florida with her husband and son. They love Mexico too. You can visit Elaine at her Web site: www.elainelandau.com.

PHOTOGRAPHS: Big Stock Photo (Alex Hinds, p. 33; Elisa Locci, p. 17; Gino Santa, p. 39; Hector Fernandez, p. 8; Jose Gil, back cover; Krzysztof Gorski, p. 15; Milan Radulovic, p. 16; Rafael Laguillo, Maya statue, p. 20; Rick Dickinson, p. 4; Stephen Sweet, p. 3; Stuart Manfred, p. 9); Getty Images (cover; p. 6; pp. 28–29; p. 31; p. 40); iStockPhoto.com (p. 30; p. 34); Photolibrary (p. 10; p. 13; pp. 24–25; p. 36; p. 38; p. 42); Stock.XCHNG (Benjamin Earwicker, p. 26; Michel Meynsbrughen, p. 18; Trish Parisy, p. 37); Stockxpert (sombrero, p. 5); Tranz/Corbis (p. 14; Montezuma II, p. 20; pp. 21–23; p. 32; p. 35; p. 41)